The Christmas Cake

An Interactive Kid's Experience with Jesus

Bev Herring

The Christmas Cake
by Bev Herring

Published 2020

This book is lovingly dedicated to
My Mother-in-law
Annie Ruth Herring
(1928-)
Whose inspiration and Godliness continues to touch people
everywhere she goes.
And Father-in-law
James Harold Herring Sr
(1927-2020)
A Soul Winner Extraordinaire

Color illustrations by:
FB.com/RavyneBlaise

It was almost Christmas Eve.

Jamie, Abby and Alex were wishing it would hurry up because their Grandma and Granddaddy would be coming over soon.

"Who wants to help me make Jesus a birthday cake?" Mom called from the kitchen.

Jamie was the first to answer, "I do!"

Both of his sisters looked up from their game in front of the Christmas tree. Why would Jamie want to bake a cake? Do seven year old boys bake cakes?

It wasn't long before all three children were in the kitchen to see what was happening.

"Can I tell the story, Mom?" asked Jamie.

"What story?" asked his sister, Abigail. She was four years old and full of curiosity.

"Do you remember what the story is about?" Mom asked Jamie as she looked in her recipe box.

"What story?" Abby asked again, "I thought you wanted to make a cake."

"The story is in the cake, Abbs," her older brother replied. "You'll find out."

"Where's the cake?" Alex questioned. She wasn't quite three but she did not like to be left out of anything.

Their mom found the recipe and pulled it from her recipe box. "First, everyone has to wash their hands before they can work in the kitchen."

Both girls took off running toward the bathrom. Jamie went over to the kitchen sink because he was tall enough to turn on the water by himself.

"Mom, please let me. I want to tell the story to the girls like you told me last year. I'm old enough. I'll be eight in January."

His mother smiled. She knew her son liked to take charge especially when his sisters were involved. "Okay, but I'll stick around to help."

As the girls came running back, Jamie said, "Okay, girls, we're going to bake a cake."

"Now, let's look at the recipe." He spread the recipe out on the table and began to read.

Birthday Cake for Jesus

Ingredients:
-1 box of Devil's Food Cake Mix (Jesus defeated the devil)
-1 Bottle of Red Food Coloring (His blood)
-1 Can of Cream Cheese Frosting (He washes us white as snow)

There is a certain age when kids love to help in the kitchen, even little boys. It affords us a great occasion for fun & an object lesson about what Jesus did for us while we bake Jesus a birthday cake. We put on our aprons, get the child or children safely to the counter and open the box of devil's food cake mix while explaining that at times we are tempted to do things we know are wrong. We want to because we were born that way...BUT Jesus made it possible to overcome this desire.

As I put the different ingredients into a bowl and allow each child to stir the mixture, we talk about how the devil likes to stir things up. BUT then Jesus was born. He came to save us from our sins when He died on a cross and shed His blood for us. As I point out the darkness of the devil's food cake mix, I open the red food coloring and pour it over the mixture and we talk about how Jesus' blood covers all our sins if we ask Him to. We put the cake in th oven.

When the cake comes out and is cooled, we gather back in the kitchen and I tell them that in the fullness of time, Jesus made a way to not just cover our sins but He gave us the ability to follow Him instead of doing what is wrong. After reading Isaiah 1:18, we talk about Jesus taking our sins away to make us white as snow as we all frost the cake with white frosting.

"Okay, Abbs, go get the devil's food cake off the pantry shelf."

Jamie could be a little bossy as a big brother, but Abby didn't hesitate this time and ran over to the pantry.

"What can I get?" asked Alex.

"Well, we need eggs, milk and a bottle of red food coloring but I'd better get all that," Jamie told her. "I know, you can get a big bowl to put everything in."

"Come on, Alex," her mother replied, "I'll help you find a bowl big enough to mix a cake in."

When all the ingredients were gathered together, Jamie began to speak in his most grown up voice.

"First, we need to take this devil's food cake
and make it according to the directions
on the package.
This is the first part of a very
important story."

He had his sisters' attention and
he was beginning to feel very important.

"You see, the devil's food cake stands for all the bad things
we've ever done."

"What does the Bible call that, Jamie?"
his mother asked.

Jamie looked up,
"Do you mean sin, Mom?"

"That's exactly what I mean" his mom said.

"Girls," he said, "This cake represents our sins."

"Yuck," said Alex.

"I don't want to eat sin," cried Abby, "This is not a very good cake."

"Hold on a minute," Jamie told his sisters as he mixed in the milk and eggs.

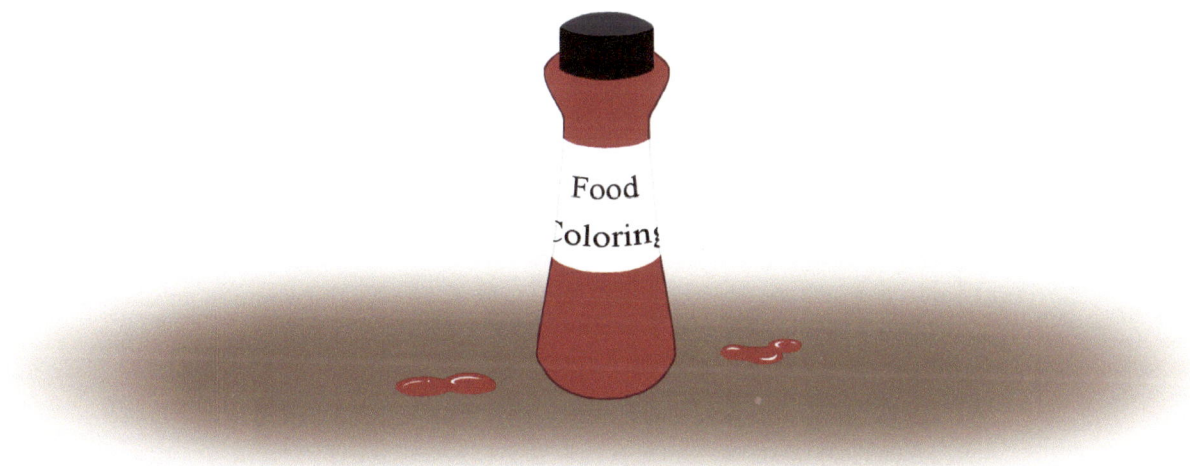

Food
Coloring

"Every time we sin, we ask Jesus to forgive us because He will. As a mater of fact, He died on the cross so we could be forgiven of our sins. The Bible says Jesus' blood makes us clean from our sins."

"Mom, hand me the red food coloring. I mean, please," he added respectfully.

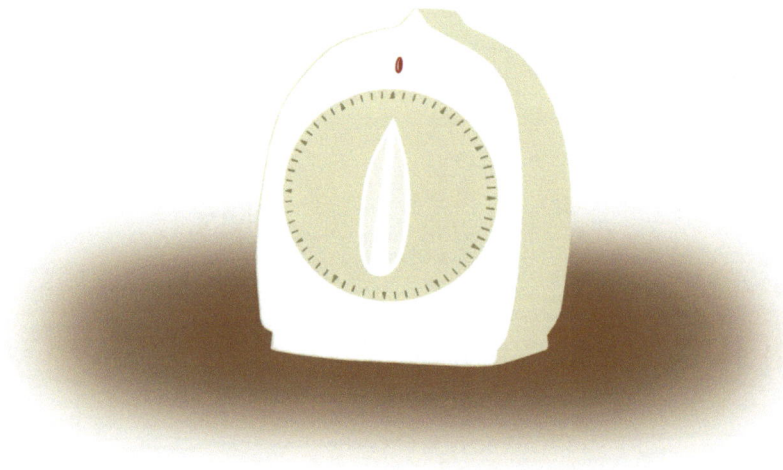

Jamie carefully opened the top and poured all the red food coloring over the devil's food cake in the bowl.

The girls peered carefully into the bowl.

As Jamie mixed all the red coloring into the cake with his spoon, his mom sprayed the cake pan with oil and checked to make sure the oven was hot.

"Okay, you three," Mom stepped over and took the mixture. Using her spatula, she made sure all the cake mix went into the pan she prepared and then put it in the oven.

"Good job, Jamie," she added. "While we wait for our cake to bake, would you like me to tell you another story?" she smiled down on the three eager faces nodding their heads yes.

Long, long ago before Jesus was
born on earth, God wanted to give
people a way to be forgiven of things
they did wrong.

God appointed priests for the temple
His people built that sat on a high hill
in the city of Jerusalem. Just down
the hill was the smaller town of
Bethlehem where the sacrficial lambs
were raised by shepherds.

Every year, there would be a search for one perfect lamb. When it was found, it would be led up the hill to Jerusalem and be led through the Sheep Gate to the Temple.

There the priests would kill a lamb as a sacrifice to take away the sins of the people.

Well, long ago Joseph and Mary

had to travel to Bethlehem

just before Jesus was born.

When they arrived,

they went from place to place looking

for somewhere to stay but all the inns

were filled with other visitors.

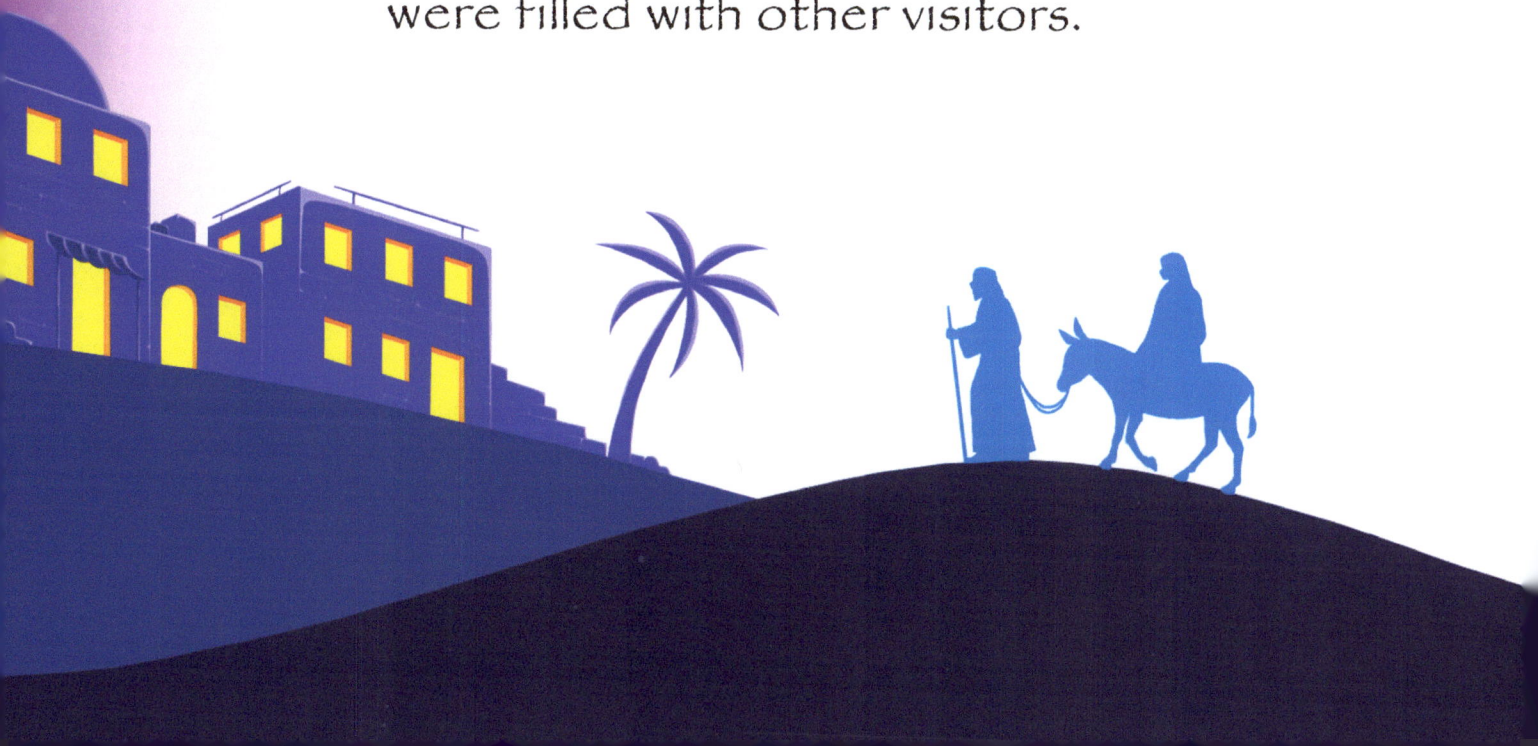

Finally, one inn keeper looked
on them with pity and
offered to let them sleep in his stable.

That night, baby Jesus was born.
Mary wrapped him in
swaddling clothes and used a
manger for his bed.

"What's a manger, Mommy?"
asked Alex.

"That is a place where food is placed
for the animals to eat,"
her mother explains.

Well, after Jesus was born there were angels that appeared in the night sky where shepherds were taking care of the sacrificial lambs.

When the angels appeared, the shepherds outside Bethlehem were told the long-awaited Messiah had arrived! And the angels even told the shepherds where to find Him.

The shepherds were so amazed they
said to one another, 'We must go to
Bethlehem and see this child.'

And just as they were told by the angel,
they found Jesus lying in a manger beside
His mother, Mary, and Joseph.

The children sat there quietly for a moment when Jamie spoke up, "Hey, Mom, the shepherds were the first ones to see Jesus even though the whole town was full of people."

"Jesus is called the Good Shepherd and the Lamb of God because He died for our sins. It must have seemed right to God to show them the Messiah first," she explained.

As the children thought about this, the oven buzzer went off.

"Oh, boy, the cake is done!" Abby said. The children hurried to the kitchen. They watched carefully as their mother removed the hot cake from the oven.

Mom spoke up, "We must let it cool for a few minutes, but, Jamie, as I fix the frosting, why don't you finish telling the girls why this cake is perfect for Jesus' Birthday."

The children gathered around their mother as she mixed the white powdered sugar, butter and milk until it became smooth.

"Remember how we made the devil's food cake mix earlier?" Jamie asked.

"I got it off the pantry shelf," added Abby.

"When I poured the red food coloring all over it until it turned red. That's because there is a Bible verse somewhere that says we become whiter than snow, right mom?" Jamie asked.

"That's true. It was spoken by the Prophet, Isaiah, in the Old Testament. He was called a prophet because God let him know things that were going to happen before they happened," their mom explained.

Isaiah said, "Come now, let us reason together, says the Lord: though your sins are like scarlet, they shall be as white as snow..." (Isaiah 1:18)

"Well, let's hurry up and put that white frosting on the cake. I want to be white as snow," cried Alex.

Everyone turned to Alex and began to laugh.

She blushed and said, "You know what I mean."

Just at that moment, they heard a car drive up outside.

"That must be Grandma and Granddaddy," shouted Jamie.

"I get to tell them the cake story!" shouted Abby as all three of them ran to the front door.

"Happy birthday, Jesus," their Mom smiled to herself.

The Christmas Cake
An Interactive Kid's Experience with Jesus

I started this tradition when my children were old enough to understand Jesus was born to save them from their sins.

There is a certain age when kids love to help in the kitchen even little boys. It affords a great occasion for fun & an object lesson about what Jesus did for us while we bake Him a birthday cake.

It's also a great way to interact with children so they experience Jesus birth through sight, sound and hands-on interaction.

About the Author:

Bev Herring is a internationally-known speaker, editor, broadcaster and Bible teacher. Bev and her husband, Harold, host a daily conference call entitled Rich Thoughts For Breakfast, part of the Debt Free Army ministry. They also own the Christian Soldier, the premiere bookstore on the East Coast.

About the Illustrator

"Ravyne Blaise" is an amazingly creative illustrator.

www.ingramcontent.com/pod-product-compliance
Lightning Source LLC
Chambersburg PA
CBHW041224040426
42443CB00003B/87